WEEKLY PRAYER JOURNAL

WRITTEN & DESIGNED BY SHALANA FRISBY

WWW.123JOURNALIT.COM

THIS JOURNAL
BELONGS TO

MY PRAYER NOTES FOR THE WEEK OF ____ TO ____

MONDAY:

TUESDAY:

WEDNESDAY:

THURSDAY:

FRIDAY:

....

....

....

....

SATURDAY:

....

....

....

....

SUNDAY:

....

....

....

....

ANSWERED PRAYERS & THINGS I'M THANKFUL FOR THIS WEEK:

MONDAY:

TUESDAY:

WEDNESDAY:

THURSDAY:

FRIDAY:

- -
- -
- -
- -

SATURDAY:

- -
- -
- -
- -

SUNDAY:

- -
- -
- -
- -

ANSWERED PRAYERS & THINGS I'M THANKFUL FOR THIS WEEK:

MONDAY:

TUESDAY:

WEDNESDAY:

THURSDAY:

FRIDAY:

- -
- -
- -
- -

SATURDAY:

- -
- -
- -
- -

SUNDAY:

- -
- -
- -
- -

ANSWERED PRAYERS & THINGS I'M THANKFUL FOR THIS WEEK:

MONDAY:

TUESDAY:

WEDNESDAY:

THURSDAY:

FRIDAY:

SATURDAY:

SUNDAY:

ANSWERED PRAYERS & THINGS I'M THANKFUL FOR THIS WEEK:

MY PRAYER NOTES FOR THE WEEK OF _____ TO _____

MONDAY:

TUESDAY:

WEDNESDAY:

THURSDAY:

FRIDAY:

SATURDAY:

SUNDAY:

ANSWERED PRAYERS & THINGS I'M THANKFUL FOR THIS WEEK:

MY PRAYER NOTES FOR THE WEEK OF _____ TO _____

MONDAY:

TUESDAY:

WEDNESDAY:

THURSDAY:

FRIDAY:

SATURDAY:

SUNDAY:

ANSWERED PRAYERS & THINGS I'M THANKFUL FOR THIS WEEK:

MY PRAYER NOTES FOR THE WEEK OF _____ TO _____

MONDAY:

TUESDAY:

WEDNESDAY:

THURSDAY:

FRIDAY:

SATURDAY:

SUNDAY:

ANSWERED PRAYERS & THINGS I'M THANKFUL FOR THIS WEEK:

MONDAY:

TUESDAY:

WEDNESDAY:

THURSDAY:

FRIDAY:

SATURDAY:

SUNDAY:

ANSWERED PRAYERS & THINGS I'M THANKFUL FOR THIS WEEK:

MY PRAYER NOTES FOR THE WEEK OF _____ TO _____

MONDAY:

TUESDAY:

WEDNESDAY:

THURSDAY:

FRIDAY:

SATURDAY:

SUNDAY:

ANSWERED PRAYERS & THINGS I'M THANKFUL FOR THIS WEEK:

MY PRAYER NOTES FOR THE WEEK OF _____ TO _____

MONDAY:

TUESDAY:

WEDNESDAY:

THURSDAY:

FRIDAY:

SATURDAY:

SUNDAY:

ANSWERED PRAYERS & THINGS I'M THANKFUL FOR THIS WEEK:

MONDAY:

TUESDAY:

WEDNESDAY:

THURSDAY:

ANSWERED PRAYERS & THINGS I'M THANKFUL FOR THIS WEEK:

MONDAY:

TUESDAY:

WEDNESDAY:

THURSDAY:

FRIDAY:

SATURDAY:

SUNDAY:

ANSWERED PRAYERS & THINGS I'M THANKFUL FOR THIS WEEK:

MONDAY:

TUESDAY:

WEDNESDAY:

THURSDAY:

FRIDAY:

SATURDAY:

SUNDAY:

ANSWERED PRAYERS & THINGS I'M THANKFUL FOR THIS WEEK:

MONDAY:

TUESDAY:

WEDNESDAY:

THURSDAY:

FRIDAY:

SATURDAY:

SUNDAY:

ANSWERED PRAYERS & THINGS I'M THANKFUL FOR THIS WEEK:

MONDAY:

TUESDAY:

WEDNESDAY:

THURSDAY:

FRIDAY:

SATURDAY:

SUNDAY:

ANSWERED PRAYERS & THINGS I'M THANKFUL FOR THIS WEEK:

MONDAY:

TUESDAY:

WEDNESDAY:

THURSDAY:

FRIDAY:

SATURDAY:

SUNDAY:

ANSWERED PRAYERS & THINGS I'M THANKFUL FOR THIS WEEK:

MY PRAYER NOTES FOR THE WEEK OF _____ TO _____

MONDAY:

TUESDAY:

WEDNESDAY:

THURSDAY:

FRIDAY:

SATURDAY:

SUNDAY:

ANSWERED PRAYERS & THINGS I'M THANKFUL FOR THIS WEEK:

MONDAY:

TUESDAY:

WEDNESDAY:

THURSDAY:

FRIDAY:

SATURDAY:

SUNDAY:

ANSWERED PRAYERS & THINGS I'M THANKFUL FOR THIS WEEK:

MY PRAYER NOTES FOR THE WEEK OF _______ TO _______

MONDAY:

TUESDAY:

WEDNESDAY:

THURSDAY:

FRIDAY:

SATURDAY:

SUNDAY:

ANSWERED PRAYERS & THINGS I'M THANKFUL FOR THIS WEEK:

____

____

____

____

____

MONDAY:

TUESDAY:

WEDNESDAY:

THURSDAY:

FRIDAY:

SATURDAY:

SUNDAY:

ANSWERED PRAYERS & THINGS I'M THANKFUL FOR THIS WEEK:

MONDAY:

TUESDAY:

WEDNESDAY:

THURSDAY:

FRIDAY:

SATURDAY:

SUNDAY:

ANSWERED PRAYERS & THINGS I'M THANKFUL FOR THIS WEEK:

MY PRAYER NOTES FOR THE WEEK OF _____ TO _____

MONDAY:

TUESDAY:

WEDNESDAY:

THURSDAY:

ANSWERED PRAYERS & THINGS I'M THANKFUL FOR THIS WEEK:

MONDAY:

TUESDAY:

WEDNESDAY:

THURSDAY:

FRIDAY:

SATURDAY:

SUNDAY:

ANSWERED PRAYERS & THINGS I'M THANKFUL FOR THIS WEEK:

MONDAY:

TUESDAY:

WEDNESDAY:

THURSDAY:

FRIDAY:

SATURDAY:

SUNDAY:

ANSWERED PRAYERS & THINGS I'M THANKFUL FOR THIS WEEK:

MONDAY:

TUESDAY:

WEDNESDAY:

THURSDAY:

FRIDAY:

SATURDAY:

SUNDAY:

ANSWERED PRAYERS & THINGS I'M THANKFUL FOR THIS WEEK:

MONDAY:

TUESDAY:

WEDNESDAY:

THURSDAY:

FRIDAY:

SATURDAY:

SUNDAY:

ANSWERED PRAYERS & THINGS I'M THANKFUL FOR THIS WEEK:

MONDAY:

TUESDAY:

WEDNESDAY:

THURSDAY:

FRIDAY:

SATURDAY:

SUNDAY:

ANSWERED PRAYERS & THINGS I'M THANKFUL FOR THIS WEEK:

MONDAY:

TUESDAY:

WEDNESDAY:

THURSDAY:

FRIDAY:

SATURDAY:

SUNDAY:

ANSWERED PRAYERS & THINGS I'M THANKFUL FOR THIS WEEK:

MY PRAYER NOTES FOR THE WEEK OF _____ TO _____

MONDAY:

TUESDAY:

WEDNESDAY:

THURSDAY:

FRIDAY:

SATURDAY:

SUNDAY:

ANSWERED PRAYERS & THINGS I'M THANKFUL FOR THIS WEEK:

MONDAY:

TUESDAY:

WEDNESDAY:

THURSDAY:

FRIDAY:

SATURDAY:

SUNDAY:

ANSWERED PRAYERS & THINGS I'M THANKFUL FOR THIS WEEK:

MONDAY:

TUESDAY:

WEDNESDAY:

THURSDAY:

FRIDAY:

SATURDAY:

SUNDAY:

ANSWERED PRAYERS & THINGS I'M THANKFUL FOR THIS WEEK:

MONDAY:

TUESDAY:

WEDNESDAY:

THURSDAY:

FRIDAY:

SATURDAY:

SUNDAY:

ANSWERED PRAYERS & THINGS I'M THANKFUL FOR THIS WEEK:

MY PRAYER NOTES FOR THE WEEK OF _______ TO _______

MONDAY:

TUESDAY:

WEDNESDAY:

THURSDAY:

FRIDAY:

SATURDAY:

SUNDAY:

ANSWERED PRAYERS & THINGS I'M THANKFUL FOR THIS WEEK:

MY PRAYER NOTES FOR THE WEEK OF _____ TO _____

MONDAY:

TUESDAY:

WEDNESDAY:

THURSDAY:

FRIDAY:

SATURDAY:

SUNDAY:

ANSWERED PRAYERS & THINGS I'M THANKFUL FOR THIS WEEK:

MONDAY:

TUESDAY:

WEDNESDAY:

THURSDAY:

FRIDAY:

SATURDAY:

SUNDAY:

ANSWERED PRAYERS & THINGS I'M THANKFUL FOR THIS WEEK:

MONDAY:

TUESDAY:

WEDNESDAY:

THURSDAY:

FRIDAY:

- -
- -
- -
- -

SATURDAY:

- -
- -
- -
- -

SUNDAY:

- -
- -
- -
- -

ANSWERED PRAYERS & THINGS I'M THANKFUL FOR THIS WEEK:

MONDAY:

TUESDAY:

WEDNESDAY:

THURSDAY:

FRIDAY:

SATURDAY:

SUNDAY:

ANSWERED PRAYERS & THINGS I'M THANKFUL FOR THIS WEEK:

MONDAY:

TUESDAY:

WEDNESDAY:

THURSDAY:

FRIDAY:

SATURDAY:

SUNDAY:

ANSWERED PRAYERS & THINGS I'M THANKFUL FOR THIS WEEK:

MY PRAYER NOTES FOR THE WEEK OF _____ TO _____

MONDAY:

TUESDAY:

WEDNESDAY:

THURSDAY:

FRIDAY:

SATURDAY:

SUNDAY:

ANSWERED PRAYERS & THINGS I'M THANKFUL FOR THIS WEEK:

MY PRAYER NOTES FOR THE WEEK OF _____ TO _____

MONDAY:

TUESDAY:

WEDNESDAY:

THURSDAY:

FRIDAY:

SATURDAY:

SUNDAY:

ANSWERED PRAYERS & THINGS I'M THANKFUL FOR THIS WEEK:

MONDAY:

TUESDAY:

WEDNESDAY:

THURSDAY:

FRIDAY:

SATURDAY:

SUNDAY:

ANSWERED PRAYERS & THINGS I'M THANKFUL FOR THIS WEEK:

____

____

____

____

____

____

MONDAY:

TUESDAY:

WEDNESDAY:

THURSDAY:

FRIDAY:

SATURDAY:

SUNDAY:

ANSWERED PRAYERS & THINGS I'M THANKFUL FOR THIS WEEK:

MONDAY:

TUESDAY:

WEDNESDAY:

THURSDAY:

FRIDAY:

SATURDAY:

SUNDAY:

ANSWERED PRAYERS & THINGS I'M THANKFUL FOR THIS WEEK:

MONDAY:

TUESDAY:

WEDNESDAY:

THURSDAY:

FRIDAY:

SATURDAY:

SUNDAY:

ANSWERED PRAYERS & THINGS I'M THANKFUL FOR THIS WEEK:

MONDAY:

TUESDAY:

WEDNESDAY:

THURSDAY:

FRIDAY:

SATURDAY:

SUNDAY:

ANSWERED PRAYERS & THINGS I'M THANKFUL FOR THIS WEEK:

MONDAY:

TUESDAY:

WEDNESDAY:

THURSDAY:

FRIDAY:

- -

- -

- -

- -

SATURDAY:

- -

- -

- -

- -

SUNDAY:

- -

- -

- -

- -

ANSWERED PRAYERS & THINGS I'M THANKFUL FOR THIS WEEK:

MY PRAYER NOTES FOR THE WEEK OF _______ TO _______

MONDAY:

TUESDAY:

WEDNESDAY:

THURSDAY:

FRIDAY:

SATURDAY:

SUNDAY:

ANSWERED PRAYERS & THINGS I'M THANKFUL FOR THIS WEEK:

MONDAY:

TUESDAY:

WEDNESDAY:

THURSDAY:

FRIDAY:

SATURDAY:

SUNDAY:

ANSWERED PRAYERS & THINGS I'M THANKFUL FOR THIS WEEK:

MONDAY:

TUESDAY:

WEDNESDAY:

THURSDAY:

FRIDAY:

SATURDAY:

SUNDAY:

ANSWERED PRAYERS & THINGS I'M THANKFUL FOR THIS WEEK:

MONDAY:

TUESDAY:

WEDNESDAY:

THURSDAY:

ANSWERED PRAYERS & THINGS I'M THANKFUL FOR THIS WEEK:

MONDAY:

TUESDAY:

WEDNESDAY:

THURSDAY:

FRIDAY:

SATURDAY:

SUNDAY:

ANSWERED PRAYERS & THINGS I'M THANKFUL FOR THIS WEEK:

MY PRAYER NOTES FOR THE WEEK OF ____ TO ____

MONDAY:

TUESDAY:

WEDNESDAY:

THURSDAY:

FRIDAY:

- -
- -
- -
- -

SATURDAY:

- -
- -
- -
- -

SUNDAY:

- -
- -
- -
- -

ANSWERED PRAYERS & THINGS I'M THANKFUL FOR THIS WEEK:

www.ingramcontent.com/pod-product-compliance
Lightning Source LLC
Chambersburg PA
CBHW021334060726

47591CB00006B/2010